Leafster

By
Sandra Kovacs Stein

**Photography by Sandra Kovacs Stein
and Alexandra Beaulieu**

Book design © 2014, BookDesignTemplates.com

ISBN-13: 978-1502460769
ISBN-10: 1502460769

Juvenile Literature, 1st Edition

Printed in the USA by CreateSpace (www.CreateSpace.com)

All things bright and beautiful,
All creatures great and small,
All things wise and wonderful,
The Lord God made them all.

(Cecil F. Alexander, *pub* 1848)

One hot poolside day when dogs sat under umbrellas to cool off...

...and little boys splashed water...

...a leafy looking bug walked up to the deck and leaped onto a bathing suit hanging out to dry.

She saw something moving at the bottom of the pool. Was it a fish?

No, not a fish. It was a small boy with dark curls.

The small boy was playing with a tall boy who had red hair on his head and on his chin.

She watched them laugh and play, and play and laugh, until shivery cold, they came out of the water to sit in the sun.

"Oh look," said the tall boy, reaching for a towel. "Look, a katydid."

The katydid walked onto his fist. It had red hair on it, like the hair on his head and on his chin.

The tall boy's dog wanted to take a look,
but she was too scared to get close.

The old gray dog wasn't scared at all.
He came over to have a sniff.

"Can I hold it?" asked the small boy, stretching out his arms.

"If you're gentle," the tall boy said. "Be careful not to hurt her."

The small boy's skin felt damp and smooth...

...as she walked up his arm...

...and down his leg.

When she got tired of walking up and down, she sat in his lap for a while.

Big brother thought the katydid was cool...

...but their little cousin said, "Eeew!"

"She's not eeew," the small boy said. "She's cute, and she tickles, and she looks like a leaf. I'm going to call her Leafster."

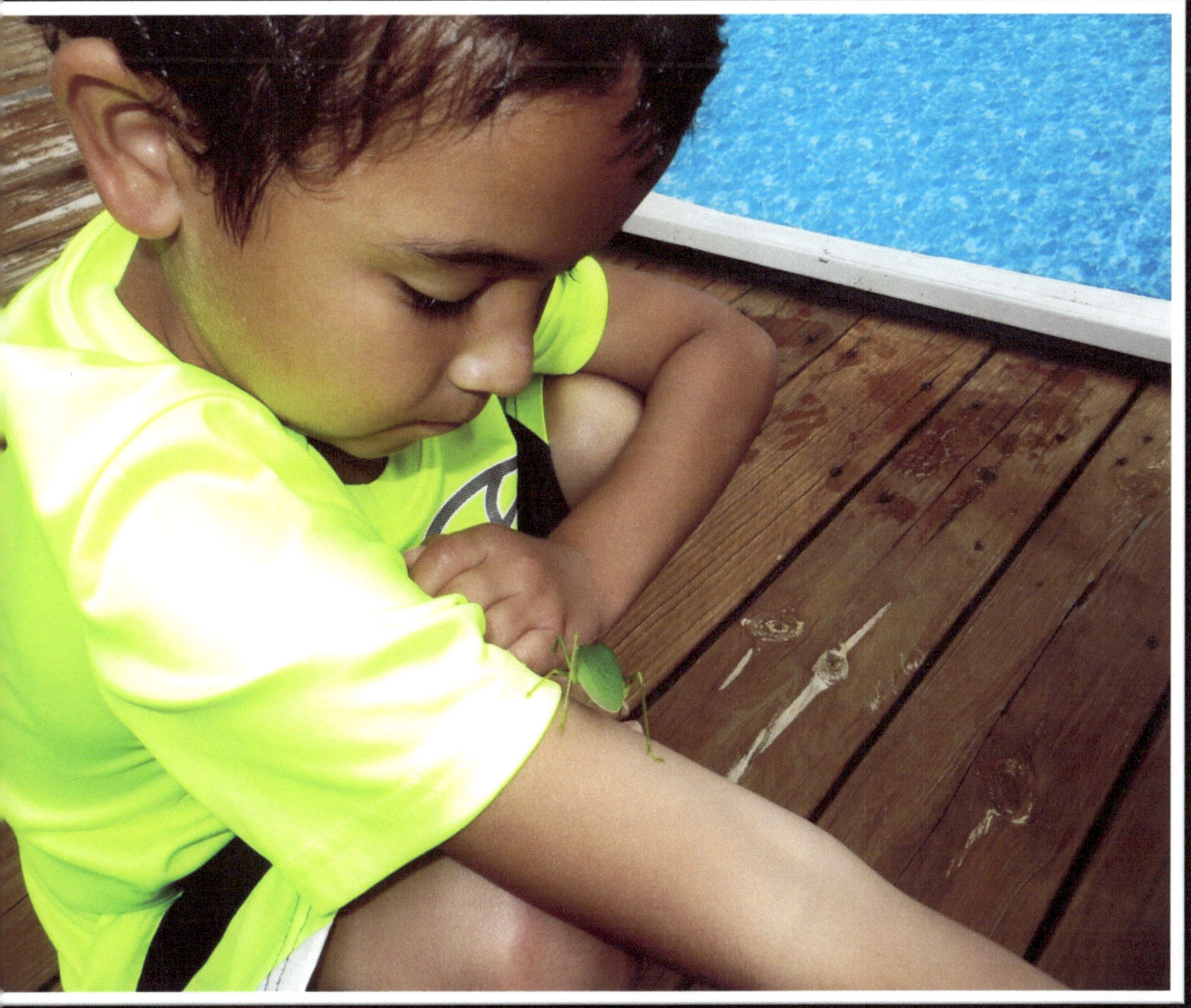

"I think she's cute too," Mom agreed.
"Look at her long antenna...

...and her sharp little tail."

Leafster and the small boy visited until the sun went down. Then she stepped onto the deck and walked back to her home on the rhododendron bush.

The End

Some Facts About Katydids

Katydids, also known as leaf bugs because of their mostly green coloring and leaf like shape, are related to crickets and grasshoppers. Some people think the sounds they make by rubbing their front wings together are like someone calling, "Katydid, Katy-didn't, Katydid, Katy-didn't," which is how they get their name.

Katydids are primarily leaf eaters, and rely on camouflage for protection, but they can also jump very quickly and very high. Their eyes are located on the sides of their head, and their long, thin antennae are used for touching and smelling. They hear through ears shaped like flat patches, tucked into the knees of their front legs.

 We know Leafster is a female because of the sharp little tail that looks like a stinger. This is a special structure used for sticking eggs into the ground or into plant stems. The eggs are laid in the fall and hatch in the spring, and the average lifespan of a katydid is about one year.

Some katydids, like Leafster, are active during the day, but most are nocturnal.

Links to Credits and Sample Sounds

- http://www.biokids.umich.edu/critters/tettigoniidae
- http://www.bugfacts.net/katydid.php#.VDNe9VdpxOU
- http://switchzoo.com/profiles/leafkatydid.htm
- http://www.fcps.edu/islandcreekes/ecology/Insects/True%20Katydid/katy1.wav
- http://entomology.ifas.ufl.edu/walker/buzz/a00samples.htm

SANDRA KOVACS STEIN is an avid photographer who enjoys taking pictures of nature and wildlife. Her career as a writer for children was launched when a pair of ravens built a nest near the top of a water tower across from her balcony in early spring 2013. They became her main subjects for months to follow, and the inspiration for her first picture book, The Water Tower Ravens.

LEAFSTER was inspired by photos Stein took of her six-year-old great-grandson befriending a katydid during a family get-together by the pool.

You can visit Stein at her photo blog, http://godsbrushstrokes.blogspot.com; or communicate with her by e-mail at skstein2010@gmail.com.

ALEXANDRA BEAULIEU is the author's granddaughter and namesake. She enjoys adventuring with her husband and documenting said adventures with her camera. She and her husband live in Wild and Wonderful West Virginia with their two dogs.